Monster Mash

Also by Susan Browne

Buddha's Dogs

Zephyr

Just Living

Monster Mash

Susan Browne

Four Way Books
Tribeca

For my parents, Robert and Jeanne, in memoriam

Copyright 2025 Susan Browne

No part of this book may be used or reproduced in any manner without written permission except in the case of brief quotations embodied in critical articles and reviews.
Library of Congress Cataloging-in-Publication Data

Names: Browne, Susan, 1952- author.
Title: Monster mash : poems / Susan Browne.
Other titles: Monster mash (Compilation)
Description: New York : Four Way Books, 2025.
Identifiers: LCCN 2024035148 (print) | LCCN 2024035149 (ebook) | ISBN 9781961897267 (trade paperback) | ISBN 9781961897274 (ebook)
Subjects: LCGFT: Poetry.
Classification: LCC PS3602.R737 M66 2025 (print) | LCC PS3602.R737 (ebook) | DDC 811/.6--dc23/eng/20240816
LC record available at https://lccn.loc.gov/2024035148
LC ebook record available at https://lccn.loc.gov/2024035149

This book is manufactured in the United States of America and printed on acid-free paper.

Four Way Books is a not-for-profit literary press. We are grateful for the assistance we receive from individual donors, public arts agencies, and private foundations including the New York State Council on the Arts, a state agency.

We are a proud member of the Community of Literary Magazines and Presses.

Contents

ONE

Science Matters 3
Air Quality Index: 500 5
Love Letters 7
Do you have children? 10
106 Degrees in Springtime 11
You Wonder If You Can Write Something 12
The Snow Doesn't Know 14
To the Future 15
Li Po's Nickname Was Immortal Exiled from Heaven 16
The Bell 17
Cayucos, California 19
Monster Mash 20

TWO

Bonanza 25
Strawberry 27
The Deal 31
Becoming a Poet 33
Little Marble Table 34
Deep Green Elegy 36
The End of the World 38
Duct Tape, Sleep, Pretzels 42
Sometimes Melancholy Leaves Me Breathless 44
Down the Lane 47
Doing It 48

THREE

Still Doing It 53
29th Anniversary 55
In the Winter of My Sixty-Seventh Year 57
& For God's Sake, Humming 60
When You Go Away 62
Covid Cleaner 63
Going Through 65

Monster Mash II   67
Torn   69
Here   71
Street Psalm   73
Romance   75

FOUR

On a Street Called Grand   79
Of a Million Earths   81
Wildflower Elegy   83
No One Except Us   85
Blue Man   86
King   87
Donovan   90
Little Altar   92
My Baby   94
After All   95
What an Idea Infinite Love   97
Blue Disco   99

ONE

Science Matters

A quantum fluctuation
Can delete the universe
In a matter of seconds
I read all about it & still don't understand
It has to do with the theory of vacuum decay
I could spend all day trying to figure that out
But I don't have time
Because in approximately four billion years
Our galaxy will collide
With the Andromeda galaxy
& both will be destroyed
& in the process form another galaxy
My father once had a Ford Galaxie
My sister almost killed us in it
Braking just in time before
We hurtled off a cliff
Afraid to move or breathe
So close to the edge
We were as silent as space
I felt a weird calm
Like knowing the universe could vanish
In less than a sneeze
Does colossal loss somehow
Ease smaller losses

But who's counting
Rivers trees starlings choking on our exhaust
I loved that car
Yellow like sunlight on wheels
I got my driver's license & the next day crunched
The Galaxie with a telephone pole
I can't remember what kind of car came next
I was starting to move into my own constellation
& my sister got married & had children who now
Have children & my parents flew past Andromeda
One fluctuation after another & what comes next
Is a subject for contemplation
At three in the morning lying in bed
Like something as cryptic as a quantum
Carried by something magnificent
We've colossally dented
No foot no brake
The cliff coming toward us

Air Quality Index: 500

On the non-day of the 8am sunset,
I went outside to put on my sandals
but couldn't find them under the ashes, the ashes
that covered the trees, the burnt furless
squirrels leaping into the charred branches.

The sky was black & orange, a ghoulish sky.
What exactly was a ghoul? I went back inside
& looked it up: *a human-like monster*
that feeds on human corpses.
I had wondered what the government was doing
during this era of cannibalism,
which had followed decades of shooting nature
seven times in the back at close range.

I needed supplies, so I put on my inferno mask
over my pandemic mask
& topped it off with my snorkel mask
against the river of cinders.
A swarm of locusts had dismantled my car.
I walked to town but it was slow going
with all the masks & my impaired leg-eye coordination.

I sat down to rest on what looked like the remains
of a scorched report from the
United Nations Intergovernmental Panel on Climate Change.
No one around. I might have welcomed a ghoul.
We'll need to get along, not be so divisive,
if we're going to save the world.
I thought about this while munching on my knee.
Getting it to my mouth wasn't difficult.
I'd been doing a lot of yoga
since being cooped up.
I took a bite out of my thigh.
A bald eagle flew by with its head on fire.

Love Letters

autumn leaves glitter in their brittling
someone plays the french horn on the shore
beneath the blue flame of sky   the sound
like silver glinting across air like tinder

dear california
when I'm gone
will you still be here
will there still be a shore

someone stomps out of the reeds
holding a fishing pole
commands the horn player to stop
I walk by into silence

missing the music
wondering what else I want
on this hot november day
a cloud spilling rain

a voice that's kind
not so many demands
not so many desires
I imagine mother earth is tired

our tumult & trash
our french horns & fishing poles
our eyelashes & elbows
our hands wanting to hold

dear humans
beautiful & dangerous
what will we do next
I keep thinking about love

about a man
who wrote to me years later
to say he was sorry for
loving badly

he was a painter
& painted me standing in a field
of wheat   wearing a yellow dress
& straw hat

like I was part of the land
the soft-gold dusk   the wind
he sees me is what I thought
I was seen

& it felt like love
it didn't last but what lasts
love lasts because here it is again
as I walk around the lake

we could have done better
we were learning   are we learning
the water is low   the color of slate
covered in crushed diamonds

the geese gliding
the hawk & falcon
the insects busy
building their empires

the snake undulating
across the road
disappearing   I see you
dear vanishings

Do you have children?

she asks as we walk off the tennis court
& someone starts up a chainsaw behind the fence

in the parking lot so I have to shout no!
& I'm suddenly tired, never been this tired

of this question that's always asked if you're a woman,
chunks of air falling around us

like wildfire monsoon oily ocean machine-gunned
atomic mushroom babies on a shriveled planet

& she yells that she has three & her first grandchild!
while we stand on the hot asphalt with that chainsaw tearing

a log to pieces & just won't quit. She opens her car door,
shows me the quilt she's made, little lambs on it

& when I touch the softness I want to be born
into a world where I say yes.

106 Degrees in Springtime

After our fight, I go for a drive
through the drought-stricken night,
stricken with how far we've come
to ruin our love, how we evolved
from monkeys to become monkeys
biting each other's throats. I want to ask the moon
for help, but its light is wilted from heatstroke.
What makes us forget that we are each other's planet
on our only planet? I park by the creek that's only a trickle.
What will we finally do with all the cars when the rivers
are dark scars, what are we doing,
I say when I get home, you standing at the door,
your sad face looking into mine, the moon
looking down on us, tearless.

You Wonder If You Can Write Something

that has hope in it.
Today, you read, there's a big rush to buy
bomb shelters.
Normal people are buying them,
not just millionaires.
There is some hope in that:
thinking life will go on after.
If you go shopping today
it won't be for a bomb shelter
but a beautiful anything
you can find: a soft pair of socks,
a necklace that catches the light
although nothing will get your mind off
of the mass grave in Ukraine,
the jawbones & eye sockets,
the pregnant women running
from the destroyed maternity hospital.
Your friend said she doesn't read the news
because what can she do, what can any of us do
to stop the butchers
because we have to be butchers
to stop them, a hopeless logic.
You could put a pear in your pocket
& pretend you have a horse to slowly feed it to.

You could build a ramshackle hut
for the dandelions before the spring wind
blows through.

The Snow Doesn't Know

The snow doesn't know when to snow anymore, we wear
wool hats & mittens at the end of June in California, no one says
freak weather anymore, the subject is moot, but the earth isn't
mute, says the crack of the glacier, says the groan
of the beached whale, says the ocean drowning in the ocean,
says the darkling, flightless beetle, says the Lake Tahoe stonefly
thrashing in the dying algae, so let's turn up the music as we drive
our cars toward the mountains, the snow hurtling against the
windshield like tiny white frogs falling from the sky, the race is on
to get to the slot machines, money falling from the metal mouths,
the clang, clang, clang like prisoners beating spoons against the
iron bars, as if now, after all, they're announcing they want to do
the right thing but don't know how, don't we know how, sunlight
strikes through the snow, leaves tremble in pain, trees speak
through their roots, we can hear them, don't say you can't hear
them, what do you say when you hear them, rising up, splitting
the ground, coming forward like an unstoppable army of
merciless angels.

To the Future

Long ago I couldn't wait to see you
in the form of berry lustrous lipstick
my mother finally let me wear
Now the world is losing every last one
of its teeth   You flail with us
as we fail at being the noble paragons
of animals   You needed more attention
than I thought   Now I can't stop thinking of you
when the hot wind blows   when the crows circle
cawing a searing warning above hills
like kindling   Last night the earth shook
as if trying to free itself from crime scene tape
Future   do you grieve for us   do you wonder when
we will take care of each other & the rainless trees
where I walk talking to myself

Li Po's Nickname Was Immortal Exiled from Heaven

Once, near the end of the 1960's, when I was stoned
in my friend Tammy's backyard, the moon talked to me.
It was more like telepathy.
The moon was polite but not crazy about us
stomping around on it in our big boots.

Moonlight on the water is beautiful,
especially if you're Li Po who drowned
while trying to embrace the image of the moon.

Or it might have been his own image
in the image of the moon.
It's hard for us to see beyond ourselves
as if caught in our own eclipse.

The moon isn't something a cow jumps over.
We don't know what it is.
Tonight, if I were a poet like Li Po,
I might say the moon is like a huge gold eye

though I'm the one looking,
my body filling with moonlight.

The Bell

I read about a newborn elephant who cried
for five hours without stopping after he was rejected by his mother.

Then I read another article about how scientists don't know for sure
if elephants cry, not 100 percent anyway & a third article argued

they probably do cry & a fourth said no, they don't.
I'm 100 percent sure we can argue about the giraffe

that remained beside the body of her one-month-old calf
for five days & about the other female giraffes joining her,

wrapping their long necks around one another in a *sort of* hug.
The article said, *they seemed to find comfort in connecting*

with one another in their shared emotions. It seems to me
that if I was looking at the five-day dead calf & those necks,

I might cry. Maybe not for five hours nonstop, but I'd probably
    shed a tear.
Or maybe I'd be crying about something else & not the giraffes,

because there's always the argument that I'm a crier, someone
    who weeps

at the least thing, like when she reads about elephants

that are so broken & beaten they need help drinking water &
eating lettuce
& taking a bath & walking on the battled earth

& about the people who do this work, people who've never
been to a dentist
who charges 2,000 dollars to fix a tooth, people with only a
few teeth left

but they use their mouths to talk to elephants, their hands to
play cards
with elephants. They walk barefoot through the forest to show
respect.

I want someone to put a bell around our necks
like they did on the elephant Raghu in case he got lost.

So we can stop arguing & hear the bell
that has been ringing & ringing.

Cayucos, California

I walk by flowers who are god
to me, dark purple yarrow, bright orange aloe,
geraniums, alliums & then the sea,
the sea, the beautiful sea!
I step onto the beach that's shrinking
as the oceans rise while I walk
in the sunset to be with the divine-
in-everything, even in us who cause the end of life.
The waves move in & out, the earth's breath.
I listen to the sandpipers' little whistles
as they gather & race into the foam
on toothpick legs. So much to love,
too much to lose as the sun sizzles
into the sea, the sea washing over
my shoes, my face stung by the wind,
the furious wind.

Monster Mash

-after the painting, "Spill (Birds)," by Julie Heffernan

Like an anxious Eve—let's call her Eve—she sits under a
massive tree
with huge red flowers as if the tree has exploded from its heart.

Snakes coil around the branches & the birds seem restless,
their wings open, in flight. Are they leaving?

A vulture perches closest to Eve while she looks up into the spill
of blood & beauty.

Her arm is raised, her hand reaching for & through a flower.
Or to ward off something coming toward her.

She straddles a branch, or is it a root? Either way, she's part of
the monstrous, radiant tree that is full of the flux of nature

& perhaps reflects the furious happenings
as we get deeper into humanity's existence.

She leans back, amazed, as if she's given birth,
her bewildered eyes wide open, witnessing.

TWO

Bonanza

Amanda shows me my bones,
A picture of my spine, ghost-like,
Snake-like, like it could rattle.
I say, *Amanda, it looks crooked, why*
Is that? She shrugs, *You're not the only one.*
Your bone density's fine. You can go now.
My plebeian spine walks me toward
The mammogram room where I flop my boob
Onto the plastic tray. Flop is not exactly accurate
Concerning these tater tots.
Darlene tussles with them, trying to yank
What's barely there & squish it under
The plate. *Wait!* I say, trying not to yell.
Darlene waits, complimenting me on my earrings.
I explain where I bought them in case she'd like a pair
& she asks if I'm ready & before I answer
My flesh is smashed & splayed into place,
I'm told not to breathe, the machine whirs,
My spine curves even more weirdly.
I am bones hung with a hunk
Of tissue muscle blood, I am not the only one
Who rattles & spins on the wheel of living's roulette
& finally Darlene says you can go now as she stares
At a computer screen. Is her expression alarmed

Or maybe her mouth's just slightly crooked? I stand
Straight & naked from the waist up except for my earrings,
The room cold slabs of concrete where the body is a dumb
Animal searching for a way out. Bloused, I elevator
From the basement & walk outside into a bonanza
Of sunshine, the crowded street, the amazing meat
Of us, the jostling bones of us, the creaking, the sloshing,
The man carrying his baby against his chest in a sash
As if he's holding eggs while riding a unicycle,
The old lady pushing an older lady in a wheelchair
So slowly the universe could be redesigned
Before they cross the street to the storefront brimming
With apricots & artichokes. Doesn't take X-ray eyes
To see something inside us all, like a secret
I wish we'd tell without fear, leaning close,
Nearly kissing the other's ear.

Strawberry

When I got my period, there wasn't any sweetness
in sitting on the toilet waiting for my mother

to return from the store with the white rowboat
I'd have to wear between my legs once a month

for the next 38 years. It was summer, the strawberries
ripe in the backyard where my father was sweeping the patio,

walking over to the bathroom window to say, "Okay in there?"
"Uh-huh," I said, shuddering in embarrassment

& lying, but who told the raw sodden biological truth?
My mother, my father, my older sister, at least one of them

might have let me in on the devastation of menstruation.
I mean, I'd heard of it like I'd heard of death—

a vague rumor or something that happened
to anyone other than me. I wasn't even sure yet

if I wanted to be a girl. Being female was a truth
I couldn't escape, but that didn't keep me from trying.

I left the baby dolls my aunts & grandmothers gave me
in the dirt while I tore around the neighborhood

with Carl & Doug, riding bikes with our shirts off & throwing
Swiss Army knives at each other's feet, seeing how close we
    could get.

I disliked curlers & cooking & sewing & women
in movies looking stupid as drool, crying when some douche

gave them a diamond ring in a glass of champagne with a
    strawberry in it.
I hated strawberries. Everybody making a big deal about how
    good

they tasted when I thought they were way too sugary & sticky
& the seeds got stuck in your teeth

& now they reminded me of my period, a word I couldn't stand,
why the hell blood dripping out of a body

was called a punctuation mark. Oh yeah, it was something
    about time

& here I was at the beginning of this cycle that would ruin every
    season,

including my favorite. How could I go swimming, wear a bathing
    suit
was all I could think about as my mother arrived & helped me
    strap on

the contraption of doom. She, to my great relief, did not say anything
as horrifying as *you're a woman now*. I would have stabbed her

with my Swiss Army knife. She tiptoed away as I sat in my bedroom,
my insides cramping like I'd swallowed a pitchfork, the sun blaring

in the window & blowing strawberries at me. A few years later, I
    was allowed
to use a tampon, but no one told me how that worked, so I
    jammed it in

with the cardboard still on & hobbled out of the bathroom, my
    legs bowed.
When I asked my sister & her friend why it didn't fit, they laughed
    so hard,

rolling around on the floor. Another soggy kind of hell while I tried
to get it out & they left for the beach.

When they returned, eating strawberry Frosty cones, I was
    reading a novel
& recovering from PTSD. I'm lying about the cones, but let's say

I took a taste anyway. I'd met a boy at a dance that summer.
It was like a line drawn in blood on the grass & I slid into another
    world.

The Deal

The doctors couldn't figure out what was wrong
in my body & in my mind, so they gave me lithium.
They thought I could be bipolar. Possibly schizophrenic.
I was 25 & afraid all the time.
The diagnosis made it hard to breathe.
My boyfriend gave me a book by a philosopher, Jiddu Krishnamurti
& went to play Frisbee.
I didn't blame him. What could he do?
I seemed to need something other people didn't need
in order to live. It amazed me how people could live.
Life felt flat as a postcard in a rusty rack in an abandoned bus
    station.
Swimming was the only relief besides crying.
I brought the lithium to the beach
& was about to take a pill
but dropped the bottle in a garbage can instead.
Not even the gulls were interested.
I made a deal: If I still felt this way in five years, I would kill myself.
Five years seemed short enough that I could bear it
& maybe long enough to heal.
Slowly, I got better.
I read the book by Krishnamurti.
He said loneliness is just loneliness. Something like that.
Once you go all the way through it, you're on the other side.

Something like that. I read the chapter over & over.
Went to hear him give a talk in an orange grove in Ojai.
His voice was a beautiful body swimming
all the way to where there is no side.
I moved north. Stood in the small yard one morning
& looked at the flowers without being scared.
The yard was half in sunlight, half in shadow.
I wasn't thinking *metaphor.* Only how precise it was.
I kneeled in the patchy grass.

Becoming a Poet

I was five,
lying facedown on my bed
when someone stabbed me in the back,
all the way through to my heart.
I screamed & my parents came running,
my father carrying me into the living room.
We sat in the chair with the high sides
like wings. I kneeled on his lap,
my arms around his neck.
My mother sat across from us,
saying, honey, it was just a bad dream.
I looked over my father's shoulder
at the dark ocean of air,
at the colorful, iridescent fish.
I tried to explain what I saw.
It's your imagination, said my father.
The fish swam like brilliant magicians
toward the window. Then they were gone.
My parents didn't know death like I did.
Or the fish, their strange beauty
my secret.

Little Marble Table

For three weeks I had a headache.
Because I was worried about my mother.

Because she had been unhappy for too long.
Because no one can be unhappy for so long without something.

So when I saw the red light blinking on the phone,
I went to the store and bought petrale sole and a box of couscous.

When I returned home, I kept my coat on while I cooked.
Because it was January and because I knew.

I kept my coat on while I ate. Because something told me to eat.
Because it might be a long time before I ate again.

Now and then, I looked at the blinking red light as if it might stop.
As if fate could take another road.

I washed the dish, the knife and fork, cleaned the stove.
The phone was on the little marble table my mother gave me.

I stood by it, my hands in my pockets.
Because of what was next.

Finally, I pushed the playback button.
A voice told me *a car, your mother.*

To *call this number,* that I should *write it down.*
The next voice said *the doctors are doing everything they can.*

And asked if anyone was there with me.
Because someone should drive me to the hospital.

Because my mind was splintered red with
Doing everything they can and *brain surgery.*

I grabbed the keys, set them down, called a friend.
I don't remember the drive.

Only that we were on the highway where it happened.
Only that everything shrank into a single point of terror.

Only that this was what my headache had warned me about.
Because I was given knowledge I could do nothing about.

Because it was an *accident.*
That word like a god swallowing a world.

Deep Green Elegy

When my mother was in a coma and they didn't know
for how long, I came home to get some clothes
and go to work for a few days.

At my apartment, I sat outside watching the sun set,
the winter blue blazing into a red so frightening
it seemed the sky was melting into the wound of itself

but I was calm, noticing the ivy growing on the fence,
the shape of each leaf, the deep dark green soothing
after the past week in the ICU where

I held onto my mother's foot through the sheet,
my older sister saying, *She's so hurt,*
my younger sister, who was in the car accident

with our mother, sitting drugged in a wheelchair,
saying, *Mom'll be okay,* our father, his face erased by tears,
only saying her name, *Jeanne.*

We believed she would live but now, alone, I knew
she was already on her way elsewhere, it was happening
as I sat in the cold although I hardly felt it,

I was somewhere else, too, inside those hearts of ivy,
going far in there as if toward
a secret I was sharing with my mother.

I lit a cigarette, I rarely smoked but usually had one
when I visited her, it was something we did together
off by ourselves in her garden, our voices drifting

like smoke, rising up into the night,
a night not unlike this one, except here the darkness
was so vast I couldn't imagine ever being afraid

of anything again. The next day,
a colleague came into my classroom
and said there was a message for me in the office

and that he would take over, and I walked down the hall
and out into the parking lot to drive to the hospital
under all that terrifying light.

The End of the World

A woman was killed by a car as she jogged across an intersection.
A friend of hers I play tennis with said, "Can you believe it?"

I put my arms around her as we stood on the court & she cried
    into my shoulder.
I didn't tell her how my mother died in a car crash after buying
    towels on sale.

You'd think we'd be used to death coming out of the blue like
    lightning
striking on a sunny day, but we're always surprised.

Then my mother's accident became a story I told so many times
as if that could bring her back. The story was like the St. Christopher
    medal

tucked safely in her purse that a policeman found in the middle of
    the freeway
& that I carried in my pocket until who knows what happened to it.

I traveled all over Europe & even went to a place, if you can
    believe it,
called The End of the World in Southern Portugal on the Vicentine
    Coast,

stood on cliffs 200 feet high & looked at what explorers thought
    was the edge
of the flat earth & I could understand why.

I was thousands of miles from home wandering beaches &
    piers, going into stone
churches when no one was there, lighting candles although
    my belief in God flitted

around like a bat in the rafters before it folded its wings &
    disappeared in the darkness.
At night in my hostel room, I ate sardines out of the tin & read
    the *Tao Te Ching,*

staining the pages with red wine & oil. The idea of the Tao was
    consoling:
An empty container that can never be emptied and can never
    be filled.

Darkness within darkness, the gateway to all understanding.
What in the world did that mean,

but it was like a kind of hope without hope so I could believe it.
A man I dated once or twice in California came to visit.

We had a beautiful time in bed. He was confused when, after
      a week,
I wanted him to leave. At the airport I apologized & kissed him
      goodbye

& we kept kissing. He said, "Why am I leaving, I can't believe this."
A few years later I realized it was because no one he loved had died.

The universe is forever out of control. The world is sacred.
I went to see my father.

In the restaurant the dining room was dark even though it was
      lunchtime,
the little candle on the table trying hard.

It had been over a year since we'd seen each other or talked
      or talked about her.
My father's eyes were sober & clear. He said, "How's the sandwich?"

We were surrounded by velvet paintings on the walls of the
      hobo clown,
Emmett Kelly, his red nose, his sad mouth, his crushed bowler hat.

In one of the paintings a monarch butterfly rested on the hat's
 brim. I decided
to take that as a sign for whatever—whether I could believe it
 or not—happened next.

Duct Tape, Sleep, Pretzels

At 35,000 feet, I look out the airplane window
& see duct tape on the propeller.
It reminds me of the human condition
& so does the curly head of the girl next to me
resting against my shoulder.
At first, it's uncomfortable
being used as a pillow
& her head is heavy, but I never sleep
on planes anyway & can still read
my book through the corkscrews of her hair.
Out the window, past the duct tape, the sky
goes on a journey of freedom
& fearlessness. That's the human condition, too,
or else no one would ever get on a plane
or have children. The girl shifts in her seat,
her head snuggles closer to my chest.
She could be my daughter
although her mother is on her other side
fast asleep. Like being fastened into sleep?
As if sleep holds you, secure.
My philosophy professor in college told the class
there was no such thing as security.
He leaned out of his chair
toward us, his face all sharp angles,

his eyes holding the softness
of frayed silk. He killed himself
before he could grade our finals.
The mother wakes up, looks at me, startled.
Oh, sorry, she says & tries to wake her daughter
with little shoves. *It's okay,* I say.
She sighs back into sleep.
I open the pack of pretzels that's been squashed
in my pocket & eat the broken pieces,
trying not to get crumbs in the girl's hair.

Sometimes Melancholy Leaves Me Breathless

3am, always 3am when I wake,
when I wish the train horn was a romantic, faraway whistle
instead of honking & hollering, the coming & going
fast & furious on each other's tracks.

All the young look so beautiful to me now,
they leave me in the dust, don't even see me, I'm less
visible to them than dust.

3am, always 3am & I try to get back to sleep
by counting my lovers, but the counting doesn't work
because I imagine my young & beautiful self plowing through
the testosterone-strewn landscape like an erotic locomotive
on a quest for the grail in the Valhalla of penises.

Out the window, scenes flash by:
a boyfriend giving me a T-shirt printed with *It's all about me.*
I put it on & break up with him. Why shouldn't it be about me?
It's been about him for centuries.

Another (sort of) boyfriend giving me a whip.
Red leather, I kid you not.
I don't remember his name but remember wondering what
     he thought

I was capable of & he was right although I didn't need the whip
to achieve it.

Oh, one of the boyfriends I loved, his dirty blond hair, his crooked
    teeth,
who I kept leaving & returning to like bringing back a rose bush
    after killing it.
We're in his backyard, among lawn chairs & beer bottles, a ratty
    Christmas tree
because it's March & he's saying he'll have no respect for himself
if we get back together.

Something to consider but look, it's spring:
pillows of green terrain, the buds drenched in bloom
as I enter another room, light lengthening across the bed,
new thighs pressed against mine, our mouths
roaming every warm hollow.

Years of this.
I'm not complaining,
but if you were sitting in your car
waiting for the train to get to its caboose,
you might be able to call yourself Methuselah.

3am, always 3am.
I lie in bed with my lives,
the one I have & the could-have-hads.
Snow geese on rice fields
like a thousand fallen stars.

Oh, the wild odds of having a life at all.
How brave it is to live, death silent within us,
the train blaring arrival & departure.

Down the Lane

Down the lane winding between & behind houses, I find the
     cottage
I rented after I left Michael, he painted it bright yellow,
     decades later
it's the same color, Mike with stars of paint in his curly black hair,
standing at the door, beer can in hand, saying, *Done,* saying,
     You sure
about this, sure as a twenty-two-year-old, he was my first lover
who I married because he asked & because of the look
in his eyes like no one could love me more, we kissed goodbye,
his smoky-sweet smell, he got into his truck, drove to Colorado, I
     went inside,
opened the windows, sat on the twin bed, only place to sit except
     a folding
chair at the scarred table where I ate mustard sandwiches, wrote
     in a spiral
notebook, read *Of Time and the River,* 900 pages, starting over
     again
when I finished, stood outside late at night, lizards darting across
the lane under streetlights, in the breeze the trees' shadows watery,
mine mixed among them, the heart young & old at once.

Doing It

The first time was on the living room floor
by the green couch in my parents' house.
When I saw what I was in for,
I questioned the logistics.
In-A-Gadda-Da-Vida
played on the stereo while I opened the Vaseline jar.
We barely got to the end of the second verse,
which included the line, *Oh, won't you come with me*
& take my hand.
An orgasm was the last thing on my mind
& it's good I didn't know that having one
would be like trying to find Amelia Earhart in Atlantis.
My boyfriend had had sex one & a half times before
& assured me as I pulled up the top of my empire dress
& stepped into my underpants with *Saturday*
stamped on the front, that doing it
would get better. I screwed the lid back on the jar
& tried to walk normally down the hall
to check on my baby sister.
She was standing in her crib, wiggling her eyebrows.
Then I heard my parents opening the front door,
saying hello to my boyfriend.
They all beamed at me when I brought out the baby,
but I was seasick, thinking about how what I'd done

made babies & how life's grand odyssey
begins on shag carpeting.
My boyfriend asked my father for my hand in marriage,
the hand with Vaseline still on it.
We all drank a glass of champagne, except for my sister.
We gave her a cigar.

THREE

Still Doing It

I know something's cooking
When you give me that look,
Your eyes appearing slightly crossed
Above your CPAP mask,
Which you start taking off,
The mask that saves you from death
By apnea but makes you look like a snorkeler
From dreamland or an escapee from a tear gas fight,
& I'm excited, but I've got my own gear to deal with,
Especially in winter, tugging off my socks & grappling
With my flannel pajamas & beret & scarf—
Yes, it's that cold in here—
Because you don't like the heat on
When you sleep & we've been arguing
About this since we met,
But we're getting fired up:
I hear the farting, whooshing sound
Of air going out of the CPAP box,
While I uncap the bottle of Sliquid,
Setting it on the windowsill,
Glancing at the label that says *botanically infused*,
Which I've learned means we won't die if we get it in our mouths,
& I negotiate the physics once again of how to shove Sliquid
    upward

As we move around enthusiastically but carefully so as not to hurt
Your disintegrating discs & pinched nerves or my sore hip &
    wrecked knee
& we're almost in place like trapeze artists
Who've had an accident
When the cat jumps up on the bed & nestles
Between my feet & I'm on top of you,
Despite my bad knee, for better aim & leverage
With one foot on its toes,
Trying to keep my meniscus from hitting the mattress
& the cat's purring & it's hard to concentrate
But by God we're going to do this
& we do it—our thirty years together not exactly disappearing
Because they're stuck on our faces—*Oh hot damn hallelujah!*
& I slowly roll off & we lie side by side
Asking each other *are you OK?*
Smiling at the ceiling, satisfied & proud
As if we've won a prize.
The cat, ignoring us as usual,
Licks her privates.

29th Anniversary

Kenneth's elbow
have I ever seen it
I mean really looked at it
I've been away on a trip &
I would like to see his elbow
& other parts
I miss his smell
sometimes cinnamon & cumin
sometimes dirty socks & popcorn
I used to think love was a coma
my mother was in a coma
from a car accident then gone
my father was in a bottle
stuffed with suicide notes
I met Kenneth a few years after
he was from Denmark
I heard a beat of a noble heart
but also like Hamlet
he said he was going to the bottom of his life
there was nothing more attractive
unfortunately I was in therapy
I said good night sweet prince centuries passed
we met again
was it fate was it chance

did you go to the bottom of your life I asked
yes he said then offered me his arm let's dance
his arm had blond hairs I felt them like furry
light all over my body
his elbow how important it is
it curved his arm around me
& I woke up for the first time
for all this time

In the Winter of My Sixty-Seventh Year

I feel the cold more
I stay in bed longer
To linger in my dreams
Where I'm young
& falling in & out of love
I couldn't imagine then
Being this old   only old people
Are this old
Looking at my friends I wonder
Wow do I look like that
Today I wore my new beanie
With the silver-grey pom-pom
& took a walk in the fog
I thought I looked cute in that hat
But nobody noticed   maybe a squirrel
Although he didn't say anything
When was the last time I got a compliment
Now it's mostly someone pointing out
I have food stuck in my teeth
Did my teeth grow   they seem bigger
& so do my feet   everything's larger
Except my lips   lipstick smudges
Outside the lines or travels to my teeth
Then there's my neck

The *wattle*   an unfortunate word
& should have never been invented
These winter months are like open coffins
For frail oldsters to fall in
I once had a student who believed
We can be any age we want
In the afterlife
I'm desperate to be fifty
Six was also a good year
I saw snow for the first time
At my great-uncle's house in Schenectady
My sister & I stood at the window
I can still remember the thrill
Of a first time   a marvel
Life would be full of firsts
I met my first love in winter
He was a hoodlum
& way too old for me   seventeen   I was fifteen
I could tell he'd had sex or something close to it
He had a burning building in his eyes
He wore a black leather jacket   so cool & greasy
Matched his hair   he broke up with me
Although there wasn't much to break
All we'd done was sit together on the bus

Breathing on each other
It was my first broken heart
I walked in the rain
Listening to *Wichita Lineman*
On my transistor radio
I need you more than want you
Which confused me but I felt it
All over my body
& that was a first too
O world of marvels
I'm entering antiquity for the first time
Ruined columns   sun-blasted walls
Dusty rubble   wind-blown husks
I'm wintering   there is nothing wrong with it
A deep field of silence
The grass grown over & now the snow

& For God's Sake, Humming

Right before the shaky architecture of the world collapsed,
before the days started stacking on top of themselves like empty
    boxes,
I was doing something as normal as sitting in Caliber Collision.
Earlier that week, I'd driven to the Sierras to see my niece
for her birthday & on the way a flying cooler
smashed into my front bumper & careened up to the windshield
breaking the glass, but I didn't drive over the cliff.
I continued up the mountain as if Zeus had offered momentary
mercy although a few weeks later no mercy for thousands,
the virus stalking.

Caliber Collision keeps calling me to bring the car in to finish
the fixing & if it's a problem, they can pick up & deliver,
they'll wear protective clothing, it'll be safe.
Safety is a pavilion made of eggshells & feathers, a cyclone
    approaching.
I was taught this by Camus & also by my mother who died in
    a car crash
while on a journey to buy towels on sale.

This morning I read an email from my student who is a single
    mother
& a recovering alcoholic with three small children at home &

60

she's so sorry
she couldn't complete her assignment this week because she's
    been hit
by depression & will try to do the work when she can
although she knows she'll lose points.
I told her not to worry about the points.

The point is I can't stop thinking about her & what can I do?
I keep thinking about spring, too, April beauty scratching your
    eyes out
& the night is full of owls who-whoing who's next. It's hard to live
even in normal times, what's normal about living,
trying to pull the arrows out from between your ribs?
I read an interview with Jack Kornfield who says he doesn't know
how long it will be, but let us do the most magnificent work we
    can do.
My husband is making a garden,
building a system for the plants so he doesn't waste water.
He's sawing wood right now & for God's sake, humming.
I thought I loved him all these years, but love doesn't come close
to what I feel for him these days.

When You Go Away

our bed's too big to sleep in
& I can't close my eyes
& I don't like what I see
me without you this body
that waited so long for yours
I miss you I missed you
until there you were
in red jeans
who wears red jeans
I'm your orphan & you're mine
it's okay we can't keep
the lawn from balding
but in the slats of the patio chairs
spiders knit shrouds come home
I'll fold your clothes I'll squeegee
the shower door & not boast
I'm the better squeegeeer
I know you have to do
the work you were meant to
but the bed thinks love's all there is
a good thing maybe the pillows singing
Smokey Robinson *ooo baby baby*
ooo baby baby

Covid Cleaner

The virus took Kenneth's job,
so he's been working in the yard
weeding, whacking, raking.

Today, he's tackling the basement
like a wrestler, hunched over because
he can't stand up in that dank space.

He sweats & hurls junk out the door into his pruned bushes.

I look through the crap we haven't looked at
for 25 years to see if there's anything worth saving
among the Rollerblades & unspooled cassette tapes
& spare tires for bikes long gone.

Were the dented suitcases with broken zippers
carrying dreams of traveling far away from mortality?
Did we hope to ride a spare tire backward
into our faded photographs?

Kenneth hulks into the house, trailing clouds of debris.
He starts in on the floors, vacuuming then getting down on his
    knees

to wash them with rags. Onward to the stove, the cupboards,
    the walls.

For lunch, he makes salmon burgers & lentil hummus & quinoa
    beet salad
& bakes bread & pickles the cucumbers & preps for dinner.
He's a one-man-band-super-hero-house-husband.
He was a chef who worked twelve hours a day, six days a week.

After eating, he falls asleep in the chair,
his uncut hair plastered to his forehead.
What's next on the list when he wakes?
Build an ark?

Going Through

Your student plagiarizes for three paragraphs
& then writes his own mercifully brief conclusion:
The author is very stereotypical in this essay her being
an angry feminist most feminists if not all
want to be men that is why there
so bitter I know because I grew up in marin county.

You stare at the "there" & think, *Now there*
is something I can fix.

& it's crucial to pour a glass of wine
because you should get away from your desk
& not write an email, saying, *So far, you have an F grade*
in the class because even though you grew up in Marin County,
you are a dumbass.

In the chair by the window in the apartment you rented
across the street from the homeless encampment,
you & your wine read the next chapter of the novel,
What Are You Going Through?
The main character is staying with a friend who has cancer.
The friend plans to commit suicide before the last ravages of
    the disease.

This book is also about climate change & the last ravages of that
    disease.
This book has great writing,
but it makes you cry in your sleep.
You wake to the river of air conditioner noise,
to smoke from the wildfires burning the hair in your nostrils,
to your husband who has just walked in the door.
He spends his days cleaning the litter box
or driving around the locked-down town,
looking for a house he can't afford or a job that doesn't exist.
He drives through the broiling afternoons, past the city limits
toward orchards of almonds & peaches.

Some days you go with him because
he wants to show you what's still possible
out by the river, the egret & geese,
the fast-moving current, that autumn is here
& there, there, there
are dark pools of coolness under the leaves.

Monster Mash II

In fifth grade
I lay like a corpse
on the table in front of the class
until I started slowly twitching
& got up & danced
to Boris Karloff singing *the monster mash,*
it was a graveyard smash.
Everyone laughed
& I did too, never thinking
I was a fool for love.
How much do we want to be loved?
More than a ton of boundless feathers.
We must do it ourselves, mostly.
Although when I return from a long trip
two friends on the tennis court say,
"We missed you!" They even repeat it,
"We missed you!"
& compliment my forehand when usually
they complain about my spin.
Don't I know by now
I'm worth more than
an Adirondack chair holding

the butts of strangers?
Some days are like a glorious goat
whose crystal earring
swings like a ghost in sunlight.

Torn

When you move to another town, your new place is smaller
& there's nowhere to put the stuffed wolverine

& during the glum days of unpacking,
you get exhausted with your history, with feeling guilty

about throwing away the photo of a friend who you haven't seen
since the two of you drank blood martinis at the Silk Road Café

& it hurts to dump the photo in the trash,
including the plastic frame with the knife scratch,

but while sorting through your collection of talking toothbrushes,
you tenderly remember the culinary discussions with your friend,

how putting a slab of meat under the saddle makes steak tartare
after approximately five hours of riding

& you go out to the garbage can to retrieve the photo,
wrapping it in torn paper

& decide to rent a storage unit
& pay monthly for the rest of your life

to keep pieces of worn-out, wept-over connections
in a dark, concrete box next to a freeway

as if they're alive because they are
still capable of the tiniest spark

& you hope they have a party
wearing the silly old hats you love.

Here

—after Arthur Sze

Here one wishes to be a fish under the dark mirror of creek water.

Here the turquoise art of swimming pools.

Here many Ford trucks, one with a sign on the back window:
Driver picks the music. Shotgun shuts his cakehole.

Here the worship of air conditioner.

Here mosquitos give hickeys.

Here one walks for miles through the famous park, thinking, *I
can live here.*

Here horses suddenly.

Here Brahms playing outside the 7-11.

Here rice, cypress, almond, Sierra Nevada beer.

Here the abandoned barn in a field the color of beach grass.

Here the train pulled into the station & the tracks disappeared
into camellias.

Here one still quakes at the curb, the nervous new kid on the block.

Here one's heart stands in a hallway wondering where one's
room is.

Here one searches for a home.

Here one misses home & tires of missing home.

Here nostalgia useless as a button in a drawer that forgot which
shirt.

Here warm wind ancient as sunset.

Here the art of magenta sky.

Here a fox in dry sage dreams of winter, a squirrel sunbathes
like a lizard, a bobcat strolls by with 108 degree August heat
in its mouth.

Here weather has the power.
Here dust like satin on one's ankles.

Here one may end the journey & return as a blue oak.

Street Psalm

I now live in the town where I lived 37 years ago
& I'm walking down Bidwell Avenue,
a narrow street by the creek, sound of dark water over rock,
scent of fennel & as the pavement turns & turns,
I can feel it in my body, my youth, the house like a small barn,
paint weathered, porch where my dog slept in the sun
that swung its gold arc over oak & cypress, little red house
with squeaky floors where I told a good man no,
where I was alone so I could think a clear thought,
where I read & wrote, each word a divining rod
as I began to build a life with my waitress apron & bicycle
that took me across town where duck hunters slapped my ass
& chowder slicked my hands, street where I told my pervy
grandfather to get out of the car & I drove my mother & grandmother
around the neighborhood as if that would change anything
then drove back, after all it was his car
& I almost crashed into him, a whiskey-eaten mammoth melting
in the middle of the street, oh, hell, get in,
the almond orchard where I ran through tunnels of dust & light,
row after row like infinity or possibility, hope's sweat glistening
& now I stand in front of a fancy house where my old place
    used to be
& a woman comes out to water her flowers, saying *good morning*

& I say *hi* & walk on as if it's nothing, a street in a world of streets,
billions of lives & dreams, the sky with a few clouds
like ghosts doing the backstroke.

Romance

I swim my laps today, slowly, slowly,
reaching my arms out & over, my fleshly oars,
the water silken on my skin, my body still able
to be a body & resting at the pool's lip,
I watch other bodies slip through the blue,
how fast the young are
& how old they become, floating, floating,
forgetting the weight of years
while palm trees sway above us,
a little wind in the fronds, children playing
in the fountains, one is crying, one is eating
a peanut butter & jelly sandwich, I'm hungry
& wonder, has everything important happened
& what is more important than this,
like a secret adventure, like an affair I'm having
with everyone I see, their soft or washboard bellies,
their flat or rounded butts, their rippling hair
or shiny domes, their fragile ankles,
their beautiful bones, all our atoms swimming, swimming
& making us visible & I shove off the wall,
reaching my arms out, embracing the whole
magic show, with ten more laps to go.

FOUR

On a Street Called Grand

The poppies orange & naked
pop out of the dirt next to the sidewalk
under the overpass.
We are more like them than not.
The world is full no matter how many towers fall.
Tragedy makes us part of each other,
makes us each other, or if not, screw you.
A woman apologized to me yesterday
for saying something cruel.
Her apology was about what she'd been going through.
The wind lifted her hair, the pretty pink strands from the blonde.
She'd feel ashamed, she said, for a long time.
I said does this mean we can play tennis again soon?
She laughed saying sure.
Maybe we needed to be enemies before we could be friends.
I once fell asleep drunk on a friend's couch that he called "the
    coffin."
The next morning I had claw marks on my cheek
from my hair clip.
I told my friend I was never having another drink.
But I was shamelessly back at it when my face didn't look like
    a tiger
tried to eat it.
If I go live on Long Island in a town named Baldwin on a street

    called Grand,

will I be different?

I was in Montauk for a day, my same self,

except I bought a T-shirt with a picture of a lighthouse on it.

The T-shirt is shrunk & faded now like an old friend.

I still sleep in it.

I remember my old father crying, saying all his friends were dead.

By then, I was more his friend than his daughter.

A beautiful thing. The poppies will outlast us.

Sometimes I think & I'm probably wrong,

there's nothing sorry about any of it.

Of a Million Earths

One million earths could fit inside the sun
The thought of a million earths

makes me want to be a bee falling asleep inside a flower
It's a fact: sometimes while gathering nectar bees get tired

& put their three pairs of legs over their five eyes
to block the sun which is halfway through its journey

of ten billion years
My mother loved sunsets at the beach

I remember once in Santa Barbara
our chairs close together on the sand

There's no way to fact-check this
or that we chewed Juicy Fruit gum

& talked about things we'd never shared before
or that I kept looking at the freckles

on her knees because they made me
feel peaceful as a bee dreaming inside a dahlia

A billion years since that day with my mother
or seems like it

Her middle name was Marie
I brought a boombox to the church to play *Ave Maria*

A cold morning although the sun was shining
on the only known planet in the universe where life exists

Wildflower Elegy

While hiking & crushing the wildflowers
that awed us, a friend & I talked about trust.

I told her I trusted maybe five people.
She smiled at her shoes covered in petals.

Jesus, Take the Wheel was a song
on the top of the country chart for six weeks.

Trust in God but tie your camel is an Arab proverb
or what Mohammed said or Rumi.

We live in a generous universe but don't take your hands
off the wheel even though sometimes the wheel comes off.

My mother's hands tried to steer her car with its flat tire
into the slow lane, trusting a lumber truck wouldn't untie

every camel. After the breathing machine was turned off,
her chest rose & fell until her life slowed & stopped.

But something invisible moved toward the ceiling. Or if grief
was making up stories again, I wanted the generous one

about the stone rolled away from the tomb. I believe
in this tree, gnarled & glowing, its bark stripped,

standing in the garden outside my room by the sea.
Let me be an ant in its branches, let me deserve one leaf.

On Easter, Mom pinned the golden brooch of a turtle to her coat.
The turtle's eyes were like the green jewels of her spirit.

I walk barefoot through wildflowers down to the beach.
A few petals cling to my ankles until the wind takes them.

No One Except Us

—for Cheryl

My older sister & I walk carefully arm-in-arm
along the broken sidewalk to shop & celebrate her birthday.
We've known each other since Salk
gave himself & his family the polio vaccine.
Since a cheeseburger cost 20 cents.
When we fall through the cracks in the sidewalk,
who will remember the time I drove her maroon Corvair backward
down the street when I was thirteen & we thought it was the
    funniest thing ever,
or how we tried to kill each other with soup spoons,
fighting over who would get the last chicken bouillon cube
    for lunch?
Who will recall her head covered in beer cans
to curl her hair, or us holding hands between our twin beds
because I was afraid of the dark?
Or how we sprinkled marijuana on Aunt Agnes's lasagna?
Where will the memory go of our mother & father
dancing in the kitchen to Frank Sinatra's *Fly Me to the Moon*?
When we disappear around the corner, never to be seen again,
no one will remember our joy as we sat in new dresses
at the National Bar in Nevada City eating crab on toast
& drinking the best drink ever, called *Daffy's Elixir*.
No one except us will remember us waking in the morning
& it's raining & we open the hotel window & tell each other a story
about the good smell of the wet earth.

Blue Man

You seem to like the kitchen best.
A few times I heard the bubbly perk
& scared & sleepy, I turned on all the lights.
No one there although once, in the hallway,
I saw you, a man dressed in blue—
bicycle shirt & shorts, even your helmet.
You didn't seem malevolent & looked surprised
when I asked, *What are you doing in my house?*
No answer as you faded away but I still felt
your presence in the air's turbulence.
Do you miss women & coffee & bicycles,
did you die on a ride? O world of accidents—
blue sky, leaves swirling beneath your tires
then you're wearing tight spandex pants
until the end of time. Dear ghost,
maybe you just want a change of clothes.

King

My father alone
in the hospice room.
I stand outside the door
looking in.
His old hands spotted
& resting on his chest,
the slow rise & fall
of the blanket.
I sit in a chair beside the bed
he won't wake from
& remember him walking past
my childhood room,
shouting *up & at 'em*
those summer mornings
when we stayed at the cabin by the river
where we swam together.
He liked to dip his fries in chocolate ice cream,
so I did, too.
He worked all the time, gone two weeks
or more each month,
selling batteries & spark plugs.
When I was eleven, I asked him what
he would be if he could be anything.
A beach bum, he said.

I worried about him spending
his nights away from us,
something so lonely about him.
He told me when I was much older,
when he was getting sober,
that he'd thought his parents loved
his brother more.
At eighteen my father went to war
& he was proud of his service,
but war, he said, was the loneliest
place of all.
When it was over
he flew from England to New York,
then took the train to California.
His mother met him at the station
& said, *Bob, you're dirty.*
I have his medal,
European African Middle Eastern Campaign
on one side & the American eagle on the other
with the dates *1941-1945*.
I have cassette tapes.
When my father was seventy-nine,
he came to my house once a week
& told me the story of his life

& I could finally listen.
My war with him was over.
Blame's loneliness
burned itself out.
I have his gold cufflinks,
crowns with a ruby in the center.
Small treasures
those afternoons,
just the two of us
drinking coffee,
eating ham & cheese on rye
with sweet mustard.

Donovan

I walk down a street called *Mountain*
although there is no mountain   only rolling hills
although hills don't really roll   & as I look
at a window display of shoes & pass by the candy store
a gasp in my head   a quake in my heart   they aren't
here   my father who loved sweets
my mother who loved shoes   & the sun shines
on a world of orphans   I quake along Mountain Street
like a rolling gasp although if someone asked
how are you I'd say fine   like most of us are
& aren't   I thought sadness was a prison
but it connects us & if a chain it should be
one of tenderness   my father died
two years ago although sometimes I say a year
a way of keeping him closer   can't do that
anymore with my mother   need math on paper   the ache
woven into each leaf although there are birds & nests
we live in a tsunami   waves of being & non-being
but I'm no philosopher standing at the counter buying
bunion pads   feeling drowned & drying
under fluorescent lights & warmed by the smile
of the clerk who blesses me with *have a great day* as I go out
to mountainless Mountain & remember Donovan's song

playing in my parents' house in the sixties *first there is*
a mountain then there is no mountain then there is

Little Altar

The Milky Way is bigger than we thought.
At least 100 billion stars.

We can't fathom things that large,
though forgiveness

doesn't take up any space, so quiet,
you don't know it's happening until

one day you're walking down the street
& there's more room inside you.

Are we bigger than we think?
Are we like a safe with a steel door

& when it gets blown open,
there's nothing, except the Milky Way?

I once lay down in the parking lot of a bank
where I'd deposited a 30,000-dollar check

from the company
whose faulty tire killed my mother.

I curled around the trunk of a little maple
trying to grow in the gravel.

The tree & I breathed together, the leaves
making a comforting sound in the breeze.

Cars came & went, I heard their tires,
my eyes filling with sky. I was part of it all, even

what I blamed, the Silver River, the Backbone of Night—
other names for our galaxy.

I had a choice. I would get up in a few minutes.
Or a lifetime.

My Baby

—for Kerry

We're looking at ourselves in a 3-way mirror,
clothes piled on the chair & hanging on the door,
we're in a frenzy, *oh that dress, what size is it,*
is there another one, let me try it, wow, gimme that bra,
omg, get it, it makes you have cleavage, if you don't get it
I'm getting it, these jeans are too tight, my butt's too big, uh-uh,
they should be tight, they aren't clown pants,

we're in grief, shopping for the first time
since our mother died, we can't think yet that she's not
coming back, that she won't suddenly appear
in the mirror, asking us which blouse, which hat,
we can still see the tilt of her head,
her hands on her hips, her wry smile
as we walk out into the mall, talking in her voice
about where to go next in a world of food courts
& fountains & pennies thrown in & tarnished wishes,
your ponytail swinging, you're only almost twenty,
you were born in May,

I drove our mother to the hospital
to have you, you were almost like my baby, my only baby,
you will always be my baby
& everything looks good on you.

After All

I go see Petunia,
a pig I met on my walk
& named when I first came here
last year when I had to move
away from my home,
my body a nest of stones. It's 2021,
more than halfway through,
these years passing by like smoke.
The mountains are on fire
but Petunia is a song
I sing over the little bridge
where water used to be,
where the ghost of rain
is buried under fallen petals.
I stand by the fence,
searching for my pig
& there she is
under her favorite tree,
a wilting oak, it's leaves broken
pieces of bronze & gold.
Petunia, solid & real,
her snout like an upside-down heart,
her mouth that I want to say
is smiling because that's how

I want to see it. After all, this
is the world. Her big softness,
her shadow cooling the grass.

What an Idea Infinite Love

the stars hang in the sky like suicides of light
when the garbage truck arrives screaming up the hill
& I remember my student who worked for Waste Management
& wrote about the dead body he found one morning
quit his job   went back to school
a friend has two funerals to go to Saturday
doesn't know which to choose   she's in-between
my mind's in-between dream & trash truck
the Tibetans say the bardo is an in-between state after death
you're bodiless yet your consciousness keeps whirring
until you blur into your next life   every day is a next
so is sleep a bardo   was I in one at faculty meetings
when the discussion turned to working harder
how this or that should have been done yesterday
my favorite time to die & float among the luminous chalk dust
bardo has something to do with karma too
deciding your next existence   you don't want to die
in ignorance   the intelligent thing is to offer everything
to infinite love when you're at the zero hour
seems a little late   should have been done yesterday
in the Himalayan tradition you always offer it
because each moment is a bardo suspended between past &
    future

what an idea infinite love   work softer
truck rumbling into silence   cat floating
around the kitchen above the bowl of milk

Blue Disco

Sunlight after three days of kiss-each-drop-of-rain as it falls
Sunlight on my hand as I take my racket out of its jacket
Sunlight on the ball like a ball of sunlight
Sunlight as we decide who'll serve first & which side
& she tells me her mother died
Alzheimer's then Covid nowhere to take her for three weeks
Too many corpses waiting to be cremated
Sunlight on her face as she says this
Sunlight on her collarbone shiny with sweat
Sunlight on the small silver hoop in her ear
On our breathing together through
Words like *I'm sorry it's okay she was 92*
Sunlight on the bench where we sit after the game
& she says yesterday she finally got her mother's ashes
& we're silent & out of the blue the Bee Gees *Stayin' Alive*
How can we help it we get up & shimmy & shake

Acknowledgments

Thank you to the editors of the following journals who have previously published poems from this collection, sometimes in different forms:

Anti-Heroin Chic, Catamaran Literary Reader, Crosswinds, Five Points, New Ohio Review, On the Seawall, Poetry, Rattle, San Diego Poetry Annual, and *The Southern Review*

Thank you to Jeff Walt and Phil Farabaugh for graciously hosting me at the Desert Rat Residency in Palm Desert, California.

Thank you to Kelli Russell Agodon and Annette Spaulding-Convy for the use of a line in my poem "Monster Mash II," which was inspired by a prompt from Two Sylvias Press' Weekly Muse.

"In the Winter of My Sixty-Seventh Year" owes a debt to W.S. Merwin's "In the Winter of My Thirty-Eighth Year."

The title of the poem, "Sometimes Melancholy Leaves Me Breathless" is a line from Mary Oliver's poem, "Sometimes."

"You Wonder If You Can Write Something" was written for *Rattle,* Poets Respond, at the start of the war in Ukraine. I wrote the poem after reading a *New York Times* article about Europeans buying bomb shelters, iodine pills, and survival guides. Thank you to Tim Green at *Rattle* for creating a weekly venue for poetry in response to public events.

"Air Quality Index: 500" is for Matthew Lippman
"You Wonder If You Can Write Something" is for Kim Addonizio
"Torn" is for Jack Krause
"Of a Million Earths" is for Patrice Shiluk
"Wildflower Elegy" is for Danielle Alexich
"Blue Disco" is for Portia Hatch

Thank you to my writing group who, for many years, have supported, inspired, and taught me: Susan Cohen, Rebecca Foust, Julia Levine, and Jeanne Wagner.

A big hug of gratitude to Matthew Lippman and his Rule of Three, and for our magical call and response exchange.

Thank you to Carl Dennis, Dorianne Laux, Diane Seuss, and Jaswinder Bolina for their support of my work.

Thank you to Karen Toloui and K. Patrick Conner for their attention to my poems and helpful comments. And for our long, beautiful friendship in the word.

Thank you to my family and friends for their love and understanding, especially my sisters, Cheryl Rossi and Kerry Schur. Thank you for always being there to laugh and cry with.

Thank you to Julie Heffernan for her amazing artwork.

Great gratitude to Martha Rhodes, Ryan Murphy, Seth Amos, Bridget Bell and everyone at Four Way Books for taking care in making my book happen, for your edits, suggestions, and faith.

To Kenneth Jensen: We're in deeper than 1,000 kisses deep. Will you sleep with me tonight? Thank you for every day.

About the Author

Susan Browne is the author of three previous poetry collections: *Buddha's Dogs*, winner of the Four Way Books Intro Prize; *Zephyr*, winner of Steel Toe Books Editor's Choice award; and *Just Living*, winner of the Catamaran Poetry Prize. Other awards include The James Dickey Poetry Prize, The Los Angeles Poetry Festival Prize, and a fellowship from the Provincetown Fine Arts Work Center. She lives in Northern California.

WE ARE ALSO GRATEFUL TO THOSE INDIVIDUALS WHO PARTICIPATED IN OUR BUILD A BOOK PROGRAM. THEY ARE:

Anonymous (14), Robert Abrams, Debra Allbery, Nancy Allen, Michael Ansara, Kathy Aponick, Jean Ball, Sally Ball, Jill Bialosky, Sophie Cabot Black, Laurel Blossom, Tommye Blount, Karen and David Blumenthal, Jonathan Blunk, Lee Briccetti, Jane Martha Brox, Mary Lou Buschi, Anthony Cappo, Carla and Steven Carlson, Robin Rosen Chang, Liza Charlesworth, Peter Coyote, Elinor Cramer, Kwame Dawes, Michael Anna de Armas, Brian Komei Dempster, Renko and Stuart Dempster, Matthew DeNichilo, Rosalynde Vas Dias, Patrick Donnelly, Charles R. Douthat, Lynn Emanuel, Blas Falconer, Laura Fjeld, Carolyn Forché, Helen Fremont and Donna Thagard, Debra Gitterman, Dorothy Tapper Goldman, Alison Granucci, Elizabeth T. Gray Jr., Naomi Guttman and Jonathan Mead, Jeffrey Harrison, KT Herr, Carlie Hoffman, Melissa Hotchkiss, Thomas and Autumn Howard, Catherine Hoyser, Elizabeth Jackson, Linda Susan Jackson, Jessica Jacobs, Deborah Jonas-Walsh, Jennifer Just, Voki Kalfayan, Maeve Kinkead, Victoria Korth, David Lee and Jamila Trindle, Rodney Terich Leonard, Howard Levy, Owen Lewis and Susan Ennis, Eve Linn, Matthew Lippman, Ralph and Mary Ann Lowen, Maja Lukic, Neal Lulofs, Anthony Lyons, Ricardo Alberto Maldonado, Trish Marshall, Donna Masini, Deborah McAlister, Carol Moldaw, Michael and Nancy Murphy, Kimberly Nunes, Matthew Olzmann and Vievee Francis, Veronica Patterson, Patrick Phillips, Robert Pinsky, Megan Pinto, Kevin Prufer, Anna Duke Reach, Paula Rhodes, Yoana Setzer, James Shalek, Soraya Shalforoosh, Peggy Shinner, Joan Silber, Jane Simon, Debra Spark, Donna Spruijt-Metz, Arlene Stang, Page Hill Starzinger, Catherine Stearns, Yerra Sugarman, Arthur Sze, Laurence Tancredi, Marjorie and Lew Tesser, Peter Turchi, Connie Voisine, Susan Walton, Martha Webster and Robert Fuentes, Calvin Wei, Allison Benis White, Lauren Yaffe, and Rolf Yngve.